SCHIRMER'S LIBRARY
OF MUSICAL CLASSICS

Vol. 1970

GEORG PHILIPP TELEMANN

Six Sonatinas

For Violin and Piano

Violin Part Edited by

ROK KLOPČIČ

G. SCHIRMER, Inc.

DISTRIBUTED BY

HAL•LEONARD®
CORPORATION

7777 W. BLUEMOUND RD. P.O. BOX 13819 MILWAUKEE, WI 53213

SIX SONATINAS
for Violin and Piano
Sonatina No. 1

Violin part edited
by Rok Klopčič

GEORG PHILIPP TELEMANN
(1681-1767)

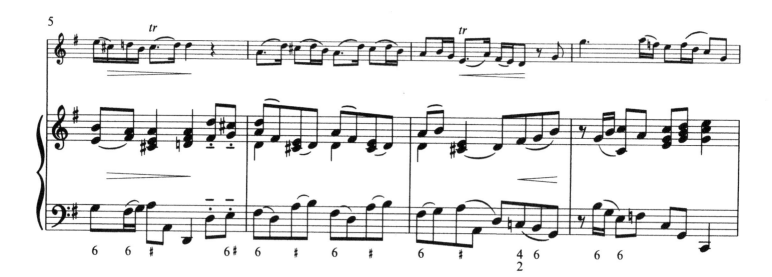

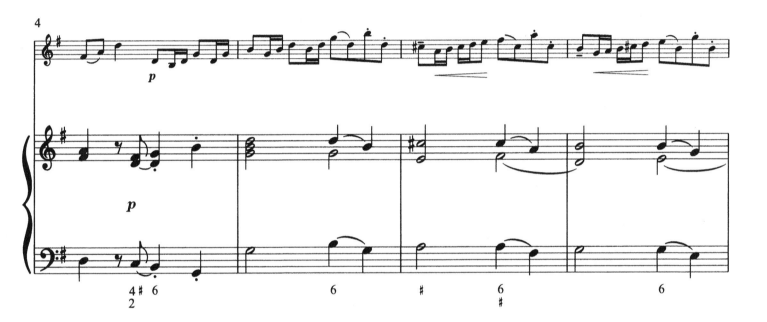

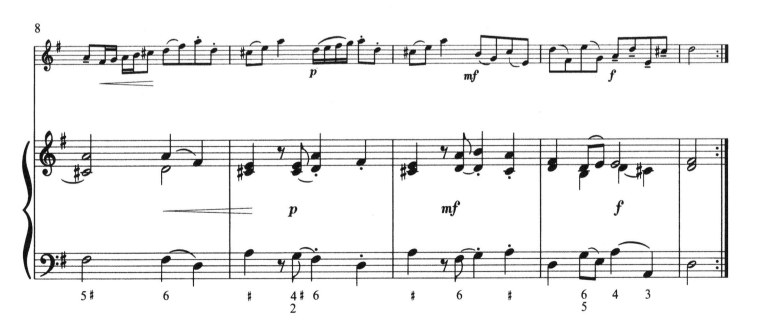

4

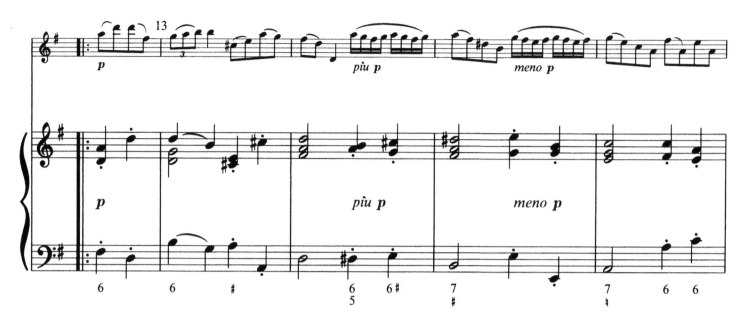

Sonatina No. 2

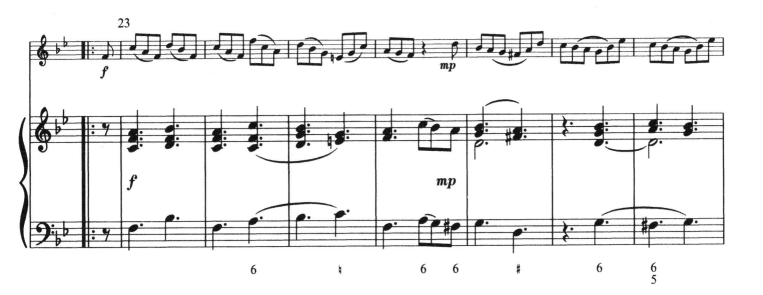

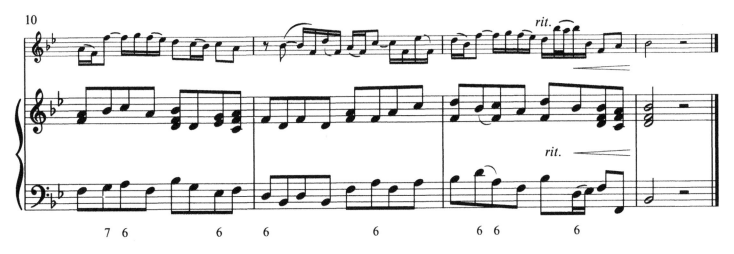

Presto

Sonatina No. 3

Largo

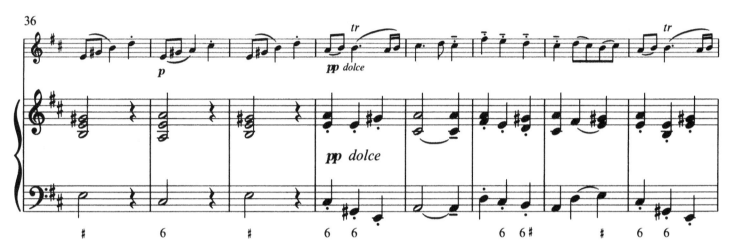

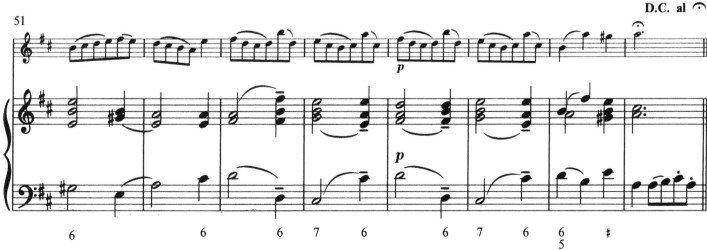

Sonatina No. 4

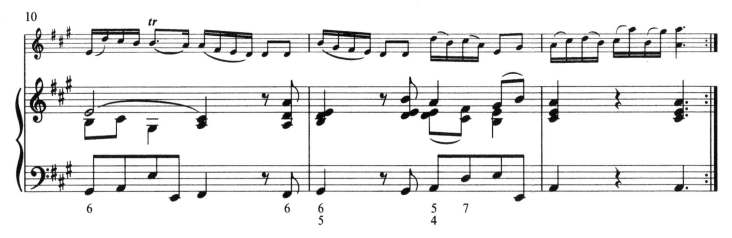

Allegro assai

Allegro

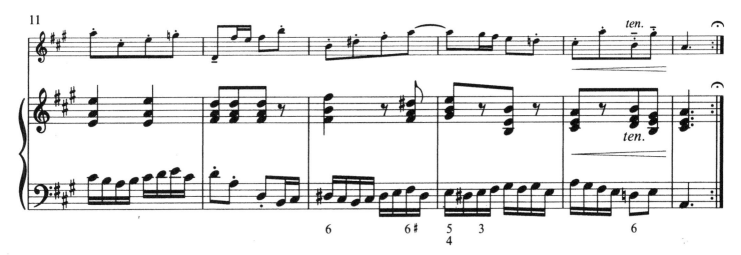

Sonatina No. 5

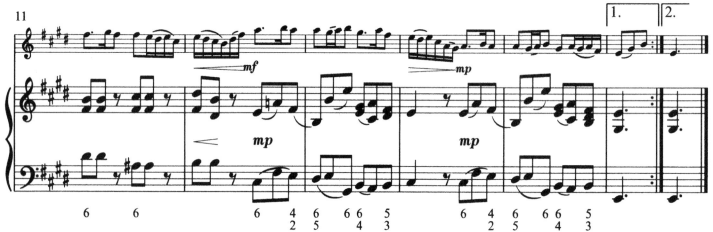

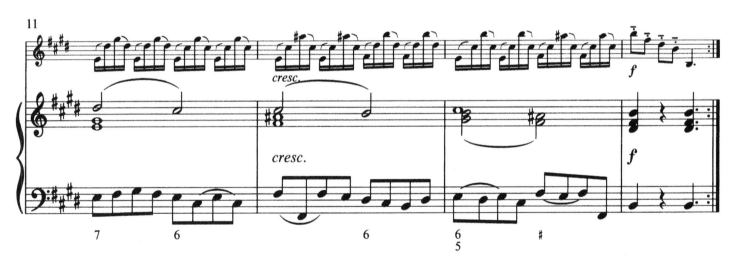

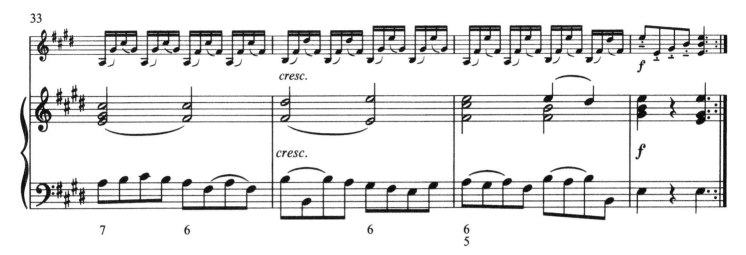

Sonatina No. 6

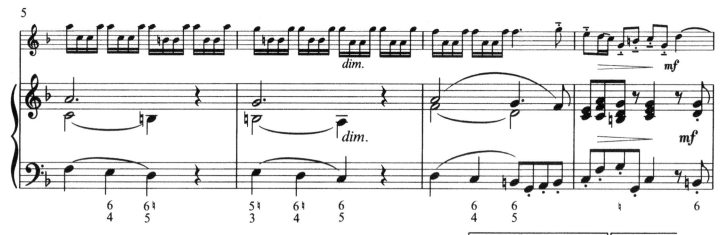

Cantabile

Presto

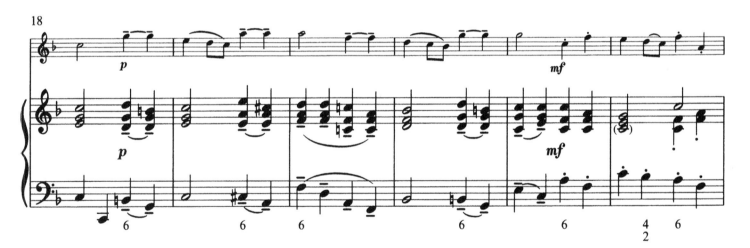

SCHIRMER'S LIBRARY
OF MUSICAL CLASSICS

Vol. 1970

GEORG PHILIPP TELEMANN

Six Sonatinas

For Violin and Piano

Violin Part Edited by

ROK KLOPČIČ

Violin

G. SCHIRMER, Inc.

DISTRIBUTED BY
HAL•LEONARD®
CORPORATION
7777 W. BLUEMOUND RD. P.O. BOX 13819 MILWAUKEE, WI 53213

SIX SONATINAS
for Violin and Piano
Sonatina No. 1

VIOLIN

Violin part edited
by Rok Klopčič

GEORG PHILIPP TELEMANN
(1681-1767)

Sonatina No. 2

VIOLIN

Affettuoso

Presto

D.C. al 𝄐

Sonatina No. 3

VIOLIN

Sonatina No. 4

VIOLIN

Largo

Allegro

Sonatina No. 5

VIOLIN

Sonatina No. 6

VIOLIN

Cantabile

Presto

SCHIRMER'S LIBRARY
OF MUSICAL CLASSICS

Vol. 1970

GEORG PHILIPP TELEMANN

Six Sonatinas

For Violin and Piano

Violin Part Edited by

ROK KLOPČIČ

Basso Continuo

G. SCHIRMER, Inc.

DISTRIBUTED BY

HAL•LEONARD®
CORPORATION

7777 W. BLUEMOUND RD. P.O. BOX 13819 MILWAUKEE, WI 53213

SIX SONATINAS
for Violin and Piano
Sonatina No. 1

BASSO CONTINUO

GEORG PHILIPP TELEMANN
(1681-1767)

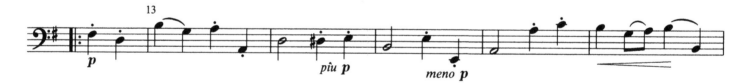

Andante

Presto

4

Sonatina No. 2

BASSO CONTINUO

36

mp

42

f

Affettuoso

48

mp

3

mp

7

10

Presto

rit.   *f*

1

7

mf

12

f   *p*

17

f   *f*

D.C. al 𝄐

Sonatina No. 3

BASSO CONTINUO

D.C. al 𝄐

Sonatina No. 4

BASSO CONTINUO

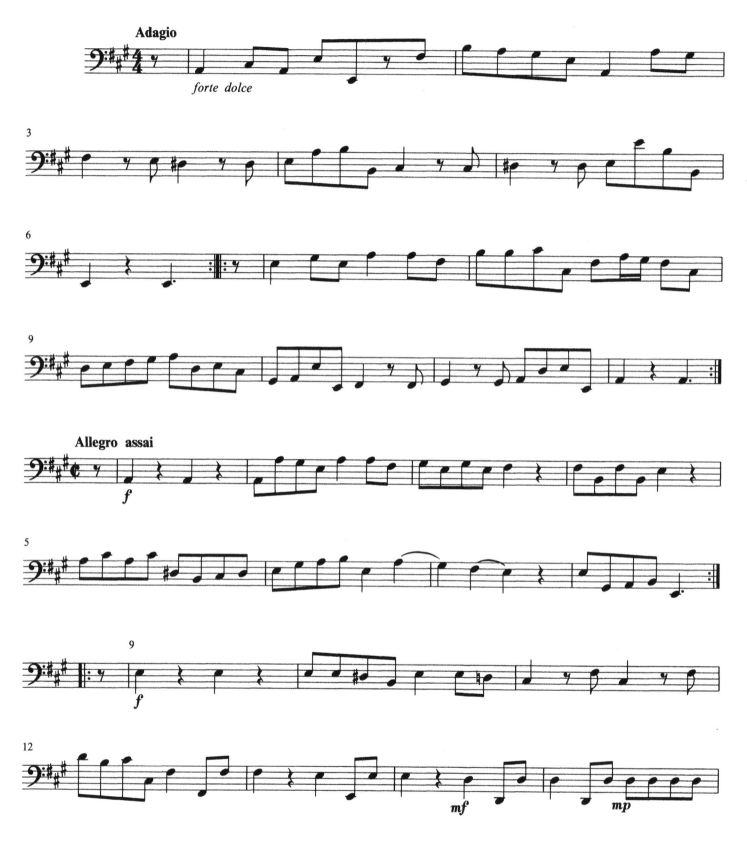

poco riten   a tempo

Largo

Allegro

Sonatina No. 5

BASSO CONTINUO

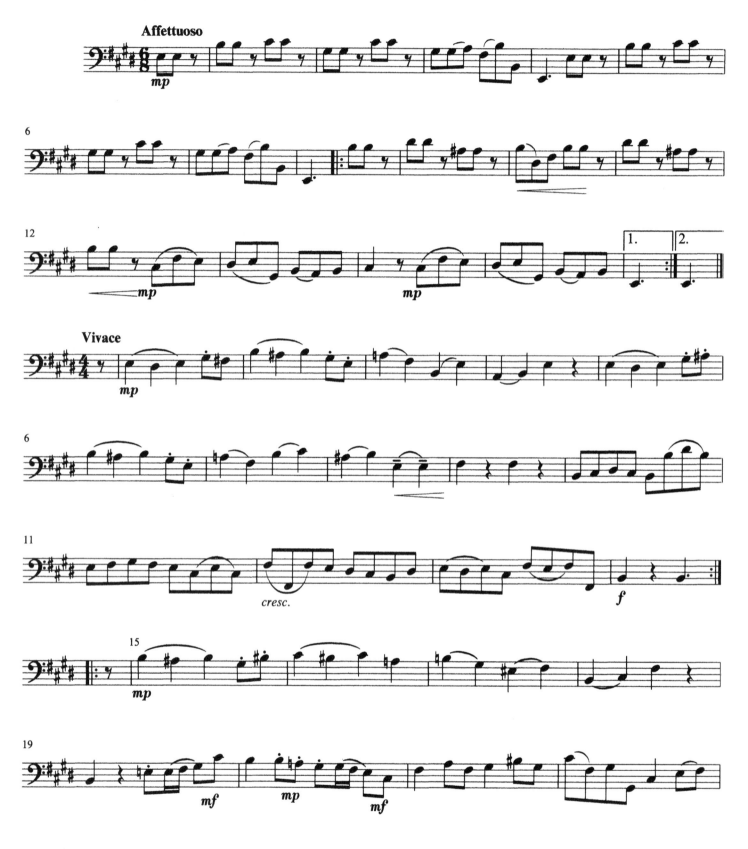

2

23

27

32

Adagio .... **Allegro**

8

17

27

37

46

55

Sonatina No. 6

BASSO CONTINUO

2